ULTIMATE
VLOGGERS'
GUIDE

If you're totally into the world of YouTube and vlogging, then this is the book for you! There's a section for each of the most popular topics on YouTube from beauty and fashion to comedy, gaming and travel. You'll find all the top vloggers within these pages. There are posters, quizzes, activities, things to make and do and of course loads of information about the stars of YouTube. Totally awesome!

TOP 10 LIFESTYLE VLOGGERS

10. SACCONEJOLYs
SUBSCRIBERS: +1.6 million
Watch them for: heart warming videos about family life.

9. NIOMI SMART
SUBSCRIBERS: +1.6 million
Watch her for: healthy lifestyle tips and serious style.

8. MYHARTO
SUBSCRIBERS: +2.5 million
Watch her for: completely honest life advice. Do not watch her for cooking tips.

7. JIM CHAPMAN
SUBSCRIBERS: +2.5 million
Watch him for: his charming manner and gentlemanly ways.

6. GRACE HELBIG
SUBSCRIBERS: +2.9 million
Watch her for: funny chatter and a sprinkling of celeb guests.

5. TANYA BURR
SUBSCRIBERS: +3.5 million
Watch her for: vlogs about the life she shares with hubby Jim.

4. SHAYTARDS
SUBSCRIBERS: +4.3 million
Watch them for: real family life.

3. POINTLESSBLOG
SUBSCRIBERS: +5.2 million
Watch him for: truly pointless but funny videos.

2. TYLER OAKLEY
SUBSCRIBERS: +8.1 million
Watch him for: funny vids, hard-hitting issues and amazing collabs.

1. MICHELLE PHAN
SUBSCRIBERS: +8.6 million
Watch her for: cool, artsy vids, clear tutorials and easy-to-follow tips.

COLOUR ME GOOD

Add some colour to top lifestyle vlogger Niomi Smart.

LIFESTYLE QUIZ

Take this quiz to find out the kind of lifestyle vloggers you should watch!

1 **What's your fave way to spend a weekend?**

a. messing around with my BFFs
b. having some relaxing 'me' time
c. spending time with my family
d. volunteering and helping others

2 **What do you enjoy reading?**

a. comics and graphic novels
b. something romantic
c. action and adventure stories
d. real life biographies

3 **Pick a social media platform...**

a. Snapchat
b. Instagram
c. Facebook
d. Tumblr

4 **What type of YouTube vids are top of your 'to watch' list?**

a. comedy
b. fashion and beauty
c. challenges
d. collabs

5 **Which job would you love to have?**

a. chat show host
b. magazine columnist
c. entertainer
d. motivational speaker

6 Which would you add to your 'watch later' list?

a. Alfie's latest vlog
b. Niomi's night-time routine
c. SHAYTARDS' daily vid
d. Tyler's 'It Gets Better' vlog

7 How would your friends describe you?

a. random and impulsive
b. sweet and kind
c. lovable and funny
d. upbeat and caring

8 Who would you love to meet?

a. Grace Helbig
b. Jim Chapman
c. Anna Saccone-Joly
d. Michelle Phan

MOSTLY As:

You love to know everything about your fave vloggers! See if they have a Snapchat account for even more insights in to their daily life.

MOSTLY Bs:

You want to watch videos that have a positive message. Whether you're watching a fashion guru or a daily vlogger, watch someone that makes you smile!

MOSTLY Cs:

YouTube is one big family, and you love to watch family life unfold online. Check out the top vlogging families for funny, unpredictable, heart-warming moments.

MOSTLY Ds:

The vloggers you love are truly inspirational. Choose your favourites when you need a confidence boost and remember: it gets better!

LIFESTYLE VLOGS

There's one thing lifestyle vloggers love to do and that's SHARE! Here are some of our favourite kinds of lifestyle vlogs. Why not make one of your own?

DAILY VLOGS

Some vloggers are brave enough to upload footage from their lives every single day, giving viewers a unique insight into everything they get up to, from hanging out with friends to shopping trips, restaurant outings, travel diaries and quality time with family.

Q&A VLOGS

Vloggers often get a lot of questions from fans – part of the problem with putting your life on the Internet is that people always want to know more! In these chatty videos, they sit-down in front of the camera to try and answer some of the questions, which range from things like 'What's your favourite pizza topping?' to more serious questions.

THE ROOM TOUR

The room tour tag is often a highly requested video, where a vlogger gives their viewers a virtual tour around their room or even their entire house. As well as getting a sneaky peek at someone else's place, room tours are a great way to get ideas on how to decorate, as well as organisation inspo, storage tips and massive motivation to tidy your own room. Seriously, who keeps their room that tidy?

THE ROUTINE

YouTube is full of 'routine' videos – night routines, school routines, routines for every season – but the morning routine video is the most popular of them all. In these videos vloggers share how they usually like to start their day, filming their each and every move, from the alarm going off to picking out the perfect outfit, checking social media, making breakfast and heading out the door.

SHHHH!

There's nothing worse than being bothered mid-way through a YouTube catch-up session, or worse - when you're busy making your own vlog! Complete this nifty door hanger DIY to keep interruptions at bay and avoid having to press that pesky pause button.

CRAFT

Instructions:
Use scissors to carefully cut along the dotted lines, decorate and display on your door handle and you're ready to vlog!

DO NOT ENTER!
I'm watching my fave vloggers!

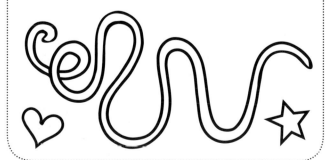

Add your own design to the blank door hanger. You could even use pics of your favourite vloggers to decorate it. If you want to make more door hangers simply trace the outline on to card, cut out and decorate. You could make one for each of your friends or one for every day of the week!

COME ON IN...
and watch YouTube with me!

LIFESTYLE WORD SEARCH

See how quickly you can find all these words about your favourite lifestyle vloggers.

Q V O H E X E R C I S E H O I
F M R E E U E Q W F I J A R F
R M O L E J I D H E L P A I I
I K F T O S L U L F G B P G T
E C U C I P O T C B F A I I N
N Z N A C V V C H D K K N R E
D R E L A X A T I O N I E A S
S Z F T Y H Y K A R L G S R S
H V V A L S J A O O L G S S O
I F S N S W A E Q O V L B S L
P B N J U H W U U Z N F I U Q
L V N U T R I T I O N N E W F R
G L N U R H F O L I V I N G E X
N D I W L K Y L N I H P L P X O
H N N E N T H U S I A S M T O

FITNESS	FASHION	MOTIVATION	EXERCISE
SOCIAL LIFE	HEALTH	FUN	RELAXATION
FRIENDSHIP	HAPPINESS	ENTHUSIASM	LIVING
BAKING	HELP	NUTRITION	

Turn to page 62 for the answers.

TOP 10 COMEDY VLOGGERS

10. SHANE DAWSON TV
SUBSCRIBERS: +7.4 million
Watch him for: music video spoofs, impersonations and hilarious commentaries.

8. FOUSEYTUBE
SUBSCRIBERS: +8.9 million
Watch him for: hilarious pranks and eye-opening social experiments.

9. IISUPERWOMANII
SUBSCRIBERS: +9 million
Watch her for: an amazing and unforgettable visit to Unicorn Island.

7. VITALYZDTV
SUBSCRIBERS: +9 million
Watch him for: some of the gutsiest pranks on YouTube.

6. PRANKvsPRANK
SUBSCRIBERS: +10 million
Watch them for: well-planned and imaginative pranks.

5. RAY WILLIAM JOHNSON
SUBSCRIBERS: +10.6 million
Watch him for: seriously witty content.

4. COLLEGEHUMOR
SUBSCRIBERS: +10.8 million
Watch them for: hilarious, original comedy.

3. JENNAMARBLES
SUBSCRIBERS: +16 million
Watch her for: hilarious and honest skits.

2. NIGAHIGA
SUBSCRIBERS: +17.3 million
Watch him for: spoofs, rants, music videos and comedy vlogs.

1. SMOSH
SUBSCRIBERS: +22.1 million
Watch them for: scripted sketches, improvisations, movie spoofs and much more!

WOULD YOU RATHER?

Tough choices ahead! Choose the options you'd prefer.

Would you rather...

1 Get pranked by VitalyzdTv?

or

Get pranked by fouseyTUBE?

2 Comb Ryan Higa's hair?

or

Pluck Shane Dawson's eyebrows?

3 Spend the whole summer with Jenna Marbles?

or

Go to Unicorn Island for one day with Lilly Singh?

4 Draw permanent cat whiskers on Zoella?

or

Play the shower prank on Joe?

5 Become part of the CollegeHumor team?

or

Hang out with Ray William Johnson?

TRUE OR FALSE?

The comedians on YouTube sometimes hide behind the crazy characters they play. Take this true or false quiz to find out how much you know about the comedy stars of YouTube.

1. The mobile app launched by Ryan Higa in 2015 is called 'Yoohoo'.

☐ True ☐ False

2. Jenna Marbles has a Masters in Sport Psychology and Counselling from Boston University.

☐ True ☐ False

3. Lilly Singh has a cameo part in 'Ice Age: Collision Course'.

☐ True ☐ False

4. FouseyTUBE started off his channel making fitness videos.

☐ True ☐ False

5. PrankvsPrank won the Shorty Award for the 'Best YouTube Ensemble' in 2016.

☐ True ☐ False

6. Fans of nigahiga are called #higalovers.

☐ True ☐ False

7. Before YouTube, VitalyzdTv wanted to be a professional skateboarder.

☐ True ☐ False

8. In 2015 Shane Dawson released a memoir titled 'I Hate Myselfie: A Collection of Essays'.

☐ True ☐ False

Turn to page 62 for the answers.

COMEDY SPEECH BUBBLE

Cut out this double-sided speech bubble and use it to add humour to your videos!

Why not write your own catchphrase on this side?

COMEDY COMIC STRIP

If you could put words into the mouths of your favourite vloggers, what would you make them say? Add your own jokes to this YouTuber comic strip.

TOP 10 BEAUTY VLOGGERS

10. PATRICIA BRIGHT
SUBSCRIBERS: +890,000
Watch her for: honest beauty advice and positive thinking.

9. FLEUR DEFORCE
SUBSCRIBERS: +1.3 million
Watch her for: on trend fashion and beauty advice.

8. LISA ELDRIDGE
SUBSCRIBERS: +1.4 million
Watch her for: tutorials on how to create modern and historical make-up looks.

7. SAMANTHA MARIA
SUBSCRIBERS: +1.7 million
Watch her for: videos full of positivity.

6. PIXIWOO
SUBSCRIBERS: +2 million
Watch them for: easy-to-follow step-by-step tutorials.

5. SPRINKLEOF GLITTER
SUBSCRIBERS: +2.4 million
Watch her for: advice, motivation, chatter, fashion and beauty tips.

4. WAYNE GOSS
SUBSCRIBERS: +2.5 million
Watch him for: top tips from one of the pros.

3. CUTEPOLISH
SUBSCRIBERS: +2.7 million
Watch her for: ideas for your next nail art sesh.

2. KANDEE JOHNSON
SUBSCRIBERS: +3.6 million
Watch her for: unbelievable make-up transformations.

1. ANDREASCHOICE
SUBSCRIBERS: +3.9 million
Watch her for: slickly edited, friendly beauty vlogs.

CASPAR MAKEOVER

Use your colouring pencils and your imagination to give Caspar Lee a makeover!

BEAUTY QUIZ

Take this quiz and discover the kind of beauty vlogger you could be!

1 What's your fave way to spend an evening?

a. watching playlists of Zoella and Alfie's collabs

b. pampering myself

c. creating nail art for my friends

d. mastering contouring techniques

2 How long does it take you to get ready for a party?

a. 10 minutes

b. 20 minutes

c. 40 minutes

d. over an hour

3 How many lipsticks do you own?

a. fewer than five

b. around 10

c. between 10 and 20

d. over 20

4 Which video would you like to make?

a. quick and easy hairstyles

b. how to choose the right foundation

c. nail art tutorial

d. fancy dress make-up transformations

5 Which YouTuber would you love to collab with?

a. AndreasChoice

b. Elle Fowler

c. Lisa Eldridge

d. KlairedelysArt

6 Pick a make-up challenge...

a. boyfriend does my make-up

b. no mirror make-up challenge

c. one product challenge

d. the power of make-up challenge

7 How many beauty vlogs do you watch each week?

a. none

b. two or three

c. around five

d. five, ten, fifteen... however many I can fit in!

8 Finally, pick an emoji:

a.

b.

c.

d.

Scoring...

For every A answer add 1 point,

for every B answer add 2 points,

for every C answer add 3 points

and for every D answer add 4 points.

My Score

1. .... = 5. .... =
2. .... = 6. .... =
3. .... = 7. .... =
4. .... = 8. .... =

TOTAL _____

BETWEEN 8-15:

You're a natural beauty and you love creating every day looks that are cute and practical. Check out Sprinkleofglitter and Fleur DeForce for stunning looks for school, work and play!

BETWEEN 16-23:

You love to create drama with your hair and make-up and choose the glam style for special occasions. Pick up top tips from glamorous YouTubers Patricia Bright and Samantha Maria.

BETWEEN 24-32:

You are an artist when it comes to make-up, and you love to have fun with your products. Try creating your own amazing transformations just like make-up guru Kandee Johnson.

BEAUTY GOALS

The beauty gurus inspire us on a daily basis to try a new technique or product, but sometimes we just wish we could be them (psst! You can totally steal their style!). Add your own beauty goals to the list below.

1. Gorgeous, healthy hair

2. Amazing nail art skills

3.

4.

5.

6.

7.

8.

9.

10.

BEAUTY CHALLENGES

The beauty gurus show their fun side, and also show off their amazing skills, by undertaking challenges. See if you can complete these challenges and prove yourself a beauty master!

FULL FACE
HIGHLIGHTER CHALLENGE

Started by beauty vlogger Mariya Lyubashevskaya this brighter-than-bright challenge sees beauty gurus layering and contouring their face using only highlighting products. Give it a try and see if you look radiant, or like a glazed glitterball.

Nailed it!   Failed it!

THREE MINUTE
MAKE-UP CHALLENGE

This is a simple challenge which sees beauty vloggers attempt to complete an entire face of make-up in three minutes, or less. Set a timer, line up your products and go-go-go!

Nailed it!   Failed it!

THE BLINDFOLDED
MAKE-UP CHALLENGE

This is the perfect collab challenge to try out with your BFF if you're brave enough. One of you wears a blindfold and attempts to create a make-up look on the other without peeking. The end result is usually pretty messy.

Nailed itl   Failed it!

MAKE-UP GAME

Are you super speedy at getting ready? Find a friend and see who can complete the make-up look first. Take it in turns to roll the dice. Look at the make-up palette opposite, and then add the matching make-up look to your beauty guru. You'll have to roll some numbers twice to complete the look. If you roll a number and you've already completed that part of the look, you miss a go!

Palette

6 - You just need to roll this once for full coverage.
5 - You'll have to roll it twice to complete the look!
4 - You'll need to roll twice, once for each cheek.
3 - There are two eyes, so you'll need to roll twice!
2 - Roll once for the top lip and once for the bottom.
1 - Roll twice to get the eyebrows perfect!

6 foundation **5** eye shadow **4** blusher **lipstick** **2** lipstick **1** eyebrows

You will need:

Colouring pencils
A dice

TOP 10 EDUCATIONAL VLOGGERS

10. BOOKSANDQUILLS
SUBSCRIBERS: +152,000
Watch her for: amazing book recommendations to expand your reading horizons.

9. THEBRAINSCOOP
SUBSCRIBERS: +340,000
Watch her for: updates from The Field Museum and taxidermy tips.

8. THNKR
SUBSCRIBERS: +671,000
Watch them for: interesting stories and opinions.

7. IT'S OKAY TO BE SMART
SUBSCRIBERS: +851,000
Watch him for: funny, relatable and easy-to-follow science.

6. CGP GREY
SUBSCRIBERS: +2.3 million
Watch him for: simple explanations to complicated issues.

5. CHARLIEISSOCOOLLIKE
SUBSCRIBERS: +2.3 million
Watch him for: his amazing short films, funny vlogs and 'Fun Science'!

4. VLOGBROTHERS
SUBSCRIBERS: +2.8 million
Watch them for: things that make nerds laugh.

3. MINUTEPHYSICS
SUBSCRIBERS: +3.4 million
Watch him for: simple explanations of the workings of the world.

2. GOOD MYTHICAL MORNING
SUBSCRIBERS: +10.6 million
Watch them for: parodies, humour and actual useful information.

1. VSAUCE
SUBSCRIBERS: +10.6 million
Watch him for: inspiring videos on a wide range of topics.

MATCH THE STATS

Since the launch of YouTube in 2005, the website has racked up an amazing amount of statistics. Can you match the stat to the fact?

33

50

40+

88

400+

80

840 MILLION+

63

1. Percentage of the world's population that uses YouTube.

2. Average viewing session in minutes.

3. Number of views for 'Charlie bit my Finger'.

4. Percentage of YouTube's views from outside of the US.

5. Number of hours of video uploaded to YouTube every minute.

6. Percentage of YouTubers on mobile.

7. Percentage of Americans on YouTube.

8. Number of local versions of YouTube.

Turn to page 62 for the answers.

SMARTY PANTS QUIZ

Take this test to find out the kind of educational vlogs you should make.

1 What's your approach to learning?

a. hands on, trial and error
b. I like to get all the facts
c. I like to do my own research
d. I like to hear other's opinions

2 Who would you love to meet?

a. Albert Einstein
b. the President of America
c. Jane Austen
d. Tutankhamen

3 If you could discover anything it would be...

a. a new galaxy
b. the truth behind the world's biggest conspiracy theories
c. Shakespeare's lost play
d. the lost city of Atlantis

4 How would you present your YouTube 'lessons'?

a. by conducting live experiments
b. by providing commentary over video footage
c. by talking directly to camera
d. through animation

5 Which YouTuber would you love to collab with?

a. thebrainscoop
b. CGP Grey
c. booksandquills
d. vlogbrothers

6 Would you rather...

a. travel to Mars
b. travel to the future
c. travel to Middle Earth
d. travel to the past

7 In your opinion, which invention is the best?

a. penicillin

b. the Internet

c. the printing press

d. the wheel

8 What's your dream job?

a. astronaut

b. politician

c. author

d. historian

MOSTLY As:
You understand the way this world works, and if you don't know something you want to find out the answer! Tackle the big questions on your science channel.

MOSTLY Bs:
You have your finger on the pulse when it comes to current affairs. Explain the big, small and important issues on your news channel.

MOSTLY Cs:
You are a total bookworm. Bring your love of books to YouTube and start your own review channel. You'll inspire your fans to try new genres and authors.

MOSTLY Ds:
If it's in the past it's interesting to you. Talk to your fans about the eras you're passionate about, whether it's the ancient Egyptians or the 1980s.

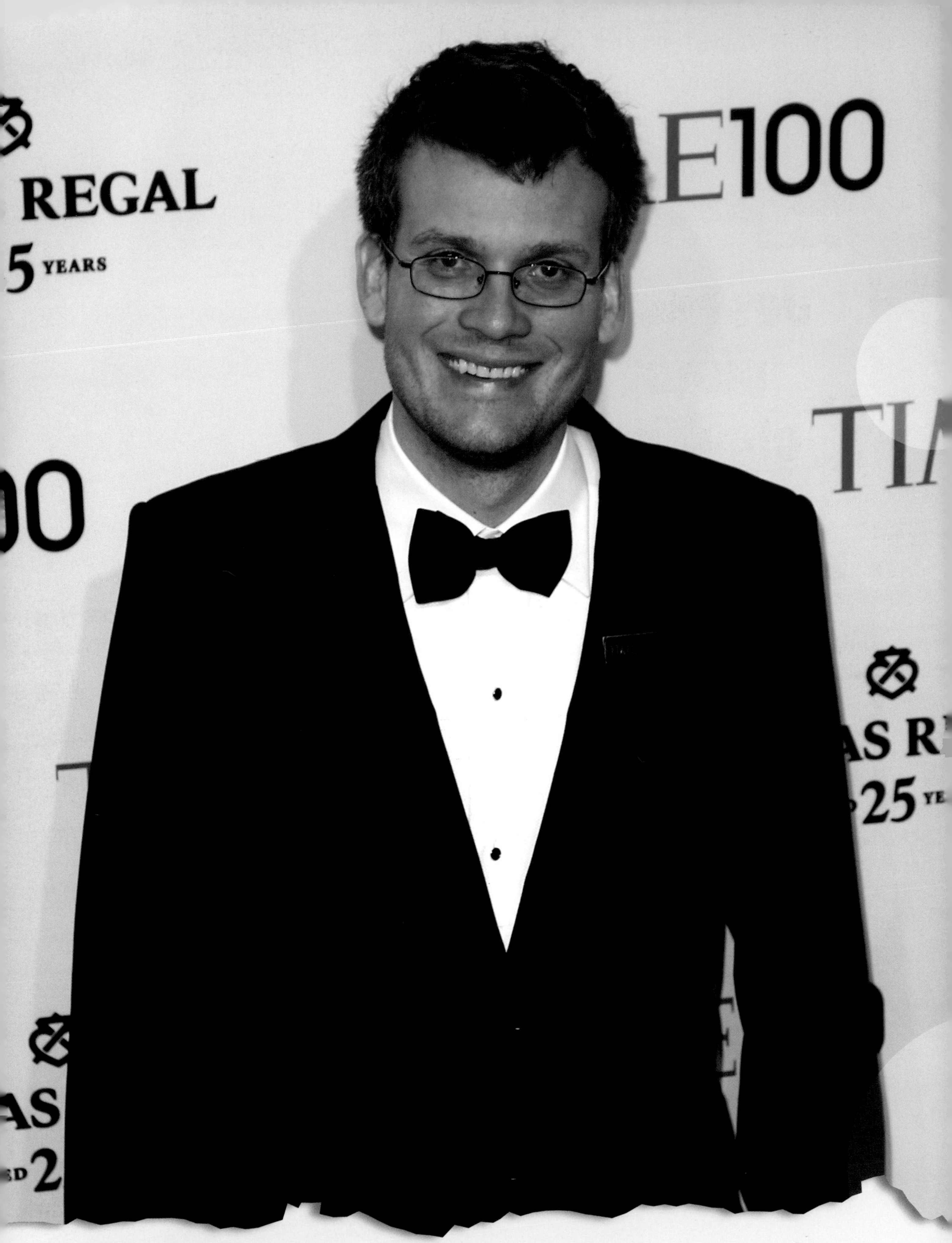
REGAL
5 YEARS
E100
25

SMARTY PANTS BOOKMARK

Colour in and create your own bookmarks. You'll need them for all the amazing vlogger books that are out this year!

Just one more chapter

Cut out and decorate these two smashing bookmarks, so you never lose the page you're on.

Make sure to use your new bookmarks when you read the latest YouTuber books!

I <3 BOOKS

VLOGGING CROSSWORD

Across

3. Which country is booksandquills from?

9. Emily Graslie aka thebrainscoop works at a museum in which US city?

10. The last name of the genius behind Vsauce.

11. Which brothers started the CrashCourse channel?

Down

1. Complete the name of Charlie McDonnell's Doctor Who-themed band: Chameleon _____.

2. What is the first name of Link from Good Mythical Morning?

4. What is the last name of the creator of MinutePhysics?

5. Which series on THNKR showcases the youngest and brightest stars?

6. Joe _____ runs the channel It's Okay To Be Smart.

7. The first name of the genius behind Vsauce.

8. Complete the title of this John Green book: 'The _____ in our Stars'.

It's rumoured that Zoella can complete a crossword in less than one minute! How quickly can you fill this one in?

TIME TAKEN

[ ] MINS

Turn to page 62 for the answers.

TOP 10 FASHION VLOGGERS

10. CLOTHESENCOUNTERS
SUBSCRIBERS: +1.6 million
Watch her for: styling tips, from bin bags to berets!

9. LAURDIY
SUBSCRIBERS: +3.5 million
Watch her for: fashion projects that even Alfie could DIY.

8. ALISHAMARIE
SUBSCRIBERS: +3.6 million
Watch her for: funny, truthful vids about life and fashion.

7. INGRID NILSEN
SUBSCRIBERS: +4 million
Watch her for: the big issues, the small issues and everything in between.

6. MEREDITH FOSTER
SUBSCRIBERS: +4.4 million
Watch her for: her fantastic back-to-school fashion tips.

5. MAYBABY
SUBSCRIBERS: +5.2 million
Watch her for: her hilarious '10 Things' videos.

4. MYLIFEASEVA
SUBSCRIBERS: +6.5 million
Watch her for: the fun side of fashion!

3. CUTIEPIEMARZIA
SUBSCRIBERS: +6.4 million
Watch her for: cute and kooky fashion ideas.

2. BETHANY MOTA
SUBSCRIBERS: +10 million
Watch her for: affordable and DIY fashion, beauty and décor tips.

1. ZOELLA
SUBSCRIBERS: +10.7 million
Watch her for: her cheery personality and amazing LookBooks.

PERSONAL STYLIST

Design an outfit for Zoella that's perfect for a day out in Brighton.

RED CARPET LOOKBOOK

Fashion vloggers love to get glammed up for red carpet events. Create your own LookBook by adding in pics of your favourite looks and designing your own outfit.

FASHION TAGS AND TRENDS

You already know that fashion tags aren't the annoying labels on new clothes. Here are some of the top fashion tag and trend videos. Check out our top tips, make some notes, and then why not try to make your own tag video?

WHAT'S IN MY BAG?

This tag is great for fashion vloggers, in fact Zoella has seven 'What's In My Bag' vlogs! It's a really easy vlog to make, as you simply pull things out of your bag and talk about what the item is!

WATCH:
Meredith Foster's 'What's in my School Bag & Essentials!'.

Write down your ideas for your 'What's In My Bag' tag vid.

_____
_____
_____
_____
_____

Draw a picture of the bag you're going to use for your vid.

OUTFITS OF THE WEEK

Share your daily fashion tips with your viewers for a whole week! This is a great video to show how you mix up your style throughout the week and lots of vloggers have created their own versions of this trend.

WATCH:
Bethany Mota's 'A Week in my Style' series.

Jot down some outfit ideas for your own week of fashion vlog!

_____
_____
_____
_____
_____

Doodle some cute accessories for your week of fashion.

GET READY WITH ME

If you've got a special event coming up, why not film yourself getting ready? This can include anything you do to relax, your beauty routine and of course how you put your outfit together!

WATCH:
Zoella's 'Get Ready With Me Festival Edition'.

Think about the different events you could film a 'GRWM' vid for.

_____

_____

_____

_____

_____

Sketch some outfit ideas for your 'GRWM' video.

CLOSET CONFIDENTIAL

Share the secrets of your closet or wardrobe with your fans. There are a series of questions to answer, so delve into your wardrobe and show your fans your fashion items!

WATCH:
CutiePieMarzia's 'Closet Confidential TAG'.

Look up the questions on Marzia's vid, and note down your answers below.

_____

_____

_____

_____

_____

Draw a pic of something you would love to have in your closet.

SEASONS OF STYLE

Which season is your favourite for fashion? Take this quiz to find out!

1 **What's your favourite type of fashion video to watch?**

a. a/w runway review
b. fashion tags
c. party GRWM vids
d. Coachella LookBooks

2 **Pick a hairstyle...**

a. messy bun
b. high ponytail
c. glamorous updo
d. long, wavy locks

3 **What's your fave colour scheme?**

a. berry shades
b. brights
c. monochrome
d. pastels

4 **Choose a holiday destination...**

a. Rome, Italy
b. Hawaii, USA
c. Reykjavik, Iceland
d. Paris, France

5 **What do you always have in your handbag?**

a. a lipstick and mirror
b. a pair of sunglasses
c. a pretty patterned scarf
d. an umbrella

6 **What's your favourite kind of party?**

a. fancy dress
b. summer wedding
c. new year's eve
d. a sleepover

7 If you could spend a day with Zoella what would you do?

a. go shopping in London

b. explore Brighton's beaches

c. ask her to give you a makeover

d. go on a day trip with the rest of the UK YT gang

8 What's the best way to accessorise a tea dress?

a. a chunky belt and knee-high boots

b. a floppy hat and oversized sunglasses

c. woolly tights and a cute cardigan

d. co-ordinated make-up and a pretty hairstyle

MOSTLY As:

You love the styles of autumn. From berry red shades to light coats and pretty scarves, keep your eyes on the catwalk for fashions to fall for.

MOSTLY Bs:

You live for the sun. Search the high street for pretty summer dresses, amazing swimsuits and totally gorgeous accessories.

MOSTLY Cs:

Winter is a season of two extremes and you love it. Think chunky knits and cosy coats to sparkly dresses for all the winter parties!

MOSTLY Ds:

The season of change is your favourite. Throw open your wardrobe doors after a long, cold winter and start wearing springtime styles.

TOP 10 GAMING VLOGGERS

10. POINTLESSBLOGGAMES
SUBSCRIBERS: +1.7 million
Watch him for: gaming fun with the UK vlog squad.

9. IJUSTINE
SUBSCRIBERS: 2.9 million
Watch her for: top advice on tech and gaming.

8. IHASCUPQUAKE
SUBSCRIBERS: +4.7 million
Watch her for: a total gaming geek out.

7. COMEDYSHORTS GAMER
SUBSCRIBERS: +6.5 million
Watch him for: hilarious cameos from his parents.

6. SMOSH GAMES
SUBSCRIBERS: +6.8 million
Watch them for: hilarious videos of good friends playing games together.

5. THESYNDICATEPROJECT
SUBSCRIBERS: +9.9 million
Watch him for: impromptu singing whilst gaming.

4. THEDIAMONDMINECART
SUBSCRIBERS: +11.3 million
Watch him for: his 'Husband vs. Wife' series.

3. KSI
SUBSCRIBERS: +13.3 million
Watch him for: hilarious Q&A Sundays with his mum and dad.

2. VANOSSGAMING
SUBSCRIBERS: +17.6 million
Watch him for: his awesome collab videos.

1. PEWDIEPIE
SUBSCRIBERS: +45.5 million
Watch him for: funny voices and hilarious faces whilst gaming.

TOP GAMES OF YOUTUBE

In 2015 YouTube released a list of the most popular games according to viewing time. Check out the list below, then write your own top 10 list.

1. Minecraft

2. Grand Theft Auto

3. League of Legends

4. Call of Duty

5. FIFA

6. Garry's Mod

7. The Sims

8. Five Nights at Freddy's

9. Puzzle & Dragons

10. Dota 2

1.

2.

3.

4.

5.

6.

7.

8.

9.

10.

PIXEL ART

Create your own level for a platform game on the grid opposite by using the pixel elements below. You could even give your new game a name!

LET'S PLAY WORD SEARCH

Before computer games there were word searches! See if you can level up and find all these gaming words in the grid below.

```
F O M E M S N S R R D P T P O
S T A R C R A F T E O U Q O E
B S L S H M A N D S O C V R R
a G K a T K M E M L N B D T F
N P L Y K E T Y L S I I Q a H
H O H G R R R a S G N O K L J
E N a M a I F O Y T F S C Y P
W G K H M U M E I N O H H I D
P a C M a N K H W D X O F a C
P N U F G N E P E M S C I Z V
U E I O O Y Z E G D a K Z E Q
O J U D O N K E Y K O N G L I
O G E B R Z R O C K B A N D S
P O K E M O N O P H B S S a R
```

SKYRIM	Halo	BIOSHOCK
FALLOUT	STARCRAFT	DONKEY KONG
ROCK BAND	PAC MAN	ZELDA
UNCHARTED	PORTAL	MYST
POKÉMON	ASTEROIDS	PONG

Turn to page 62 for the answers.

DESIGN A GAME

YouTube gamers such as PewDiePie have influenced the game industry. Imagine you're a top gamer and you get to invent your own game. Design a cover below and make some notes of how the game would work.

TOP 10 MUSIC VLOGGERS

10. DODDLEODDLE
SUBSCRIBERS: +552,000
Watch her for: catchy ukulele originals and amazing covers.

9. ITSWAYPASTMYBEDTIM
SUBSCRIBERS: +626,000
Watch her for: covers, originals and life advice.

8. SUPERFRUIT
SUBSCRIBERS: +2 million
Watch them for: spontaneous singing, amazing harmonies and superstar collabs.

7. CHRISTINA GRIMMIE
SUBSCRIBERS: +3.6 million
Watch her for: true talent. Christina's life was cut tragical short in June 2016, but her memory and music lives on.

6. PAINT
SUBSCRIBERS: +3.5 million
Watch him for: hilarious pop-culture parody sung perfectly.

5. TROYE SIVAN
SUBSCRIBERS: +4.2 million
Watch him for: amazing music that will change your life.

4. THEPIANOGUYS
SUBSCRIBERS: +4.8 million
Watch them for: classical interpretations of modern songs with plenty of attitude.

3. MIRANDA SINGS
SUBSCRIBERS: +6.5 million
Watch her for: bad dancing, awful singing and terrible advice.

2. LINDSEY STIRLING
SUBSCRIBERS: +8.1 million
Watch her for: beautifully shot videos and violin dancing.

1. PTXOFFICIAL
SUBSCRIBERS: +10.7 million
Watch them for: a cappella versions of the best songs of the moment.

YOUTUBE MUSIC QUIZ

Take this quiz to find out the kind of musical sensation you could be on YouTube!

1 Can you sing?

a. yes, I'm pretty good
b. no, but I like to try
c. yes, but I'm not confident
d. no, I'm terrible

2 Do you play an instrument?

a. my voice is my instrument
b. I do, I've been learning for a long time
c. I can but I'm not a rockstar yet
d. I tried once...

3 Have you ever performed in front of an audience?

a. I perform regularly
b. yes, as part of an orchestra
c. I've been in school shows
d. no and there's no chance I will

4 Pick an artist or band...

a. Adele
b. Louis Armstrong
c. Little Mix
d. I couldn't choose

5 Who would you love to collab with?

a. Dodie Clark
b. Lindsey Stirling
c. Pentatonix
d. The Needle Drop

6. What would you rather go to see?

a. a West End musical

b. an orchestra

c. a concert at an arena

d. an intimate indie gig

7. What do your friends think of your musical ambitions?

a. they totally support me

b. they love to jam with me

c. they sing along with me

d. they would laugh if I said I wanted to be a musician

8. Which award would you most likely win at the Grammys?

a. 'Best Solo Performance'

b. 'Best Instrumental Composition'

c. 'Best Group Performance'

d. 'Best Album Notes'

MOSTLY As:
You have the talent to become a singer/songwriter. Make sure you write songs about things you and your fans care about and watch your subscriber numbers grow!

MOSTLY Bs:
You might not have the most pleasing vocal cords but you will wow your fans on your chosen instrument. Keep practising and you could be as big as Lindsey Stirling!

MOSTLY Cs:
You have a truly talented bunch of friends. Form a covers group and bring your own sound to the songs you sing. You'll soon get noticed!

MOSTLY Ds:
You love music, but you have no musical bones in your body. Use your knowledge to become a music reviewer and give your fans your top recommendations.

LYRICS QUIZ

Do you know the words to all the original YouTube songs? See if you can complete the lyrics below!

1 Lift your legs up high,
Poke your neighbour in the eye,

....

....

Miranda Sings, 'DO THE MIRANDA'/
YouTube

2 Oh, I'm afraid of the things in my brain

....

....

Dodie Clark, 'Intertwined'/YouTube

3 I loved being a princess down in this beautiful ocean blue

....

....

Paint, 'After Ever After'/YouTube

4 And I don't want to let this go, I don't want to lose control,

....

Troye Sivan, 'The Fault in our Stars'/
YouTube

5 This human race explores space and the sea,

....

Carrie Hope Fletcher, 'I Can't Sleep'/
YouTube

Turn to page 62 for the answers.

TRUE OR FALSE?

You'll need to be a true music fan to sort the fact from the fiction in this quiz.

1. ThePianoGuys use only one instrument – the piano.

True   False

2. Carrie Hope Fletcher's brother is the drummer for McFly.

True   False

3. Troye Sivan made his film debut in X-Men Origins: Wolverine.

True   False

4. PTXofficial is an a capella group meaning they use their voices and no instruments.

True   False

5. Miranda Sings started her YouTube channel because she was deadly serious about becoming a singer.

True   False

6. Jon Cozart's first big hit on YouTube was 'After Ever After'.

True   False

7. Lindsey Stirling was voted off 'America's Got Talent' in the 2010 finals.

True   False

8. Dodie Clark is best known for playing the violin.

True   False

Turn to page 62 for the answers.

TOP 10 TRAVEL VLOGGERS

10. Brooke Saward
SUBSCRIBERS: +29,000
Watch her for: top travel tips, tricks and advice.

9. KRISTEN SARAH
SUBSCRIBERS: +80,000
Watch her for: off-the-beaten-track vlogs.

8. VAGABROTHERS
SUBSCRIBERS: +109,000
Watch them for: encounters with inspirational characters from all around the globe.

7. HEY NADINE
SUBSCRIBERS: +256,000
Watch her for: complete wanderlust inspiration.

6. HIGH ON LIFE
SUBSCRIBERS: +285,000
Watch them for: the entertaining travels of three friends.

5. MR BEN BROWN
SUBSCRIBERS: +560,000
Watch him for: laid back lifestyle and travel vlogs.

4. FUNFORLOUIS
SUBSCRIBERS: +1.8 million
Watch him for: vlogs that take you around the world.

3. CASEYNEISTAT
SUBSCRIBERS: +3.4 million
Watch him for: travel and adventure, whether it's in his home town or overseas.

2. DEVINSUPERTRAMP
SUBSCRIBERS: +4.1 million
Watch him for: some of the most amazing vids you'll ever see.

1. JACKSGAP
SUBSCRIBERS: +4.2 million
Watch them for: fun videos from YouTube's cheekiest siblings.

TRAVEL BUCKET LIST

What's on your bucket list? Fill this list with the places you really want to go and the adventures you want to have. We've started you off!

1. Visit New York
2. Learn to surf
3. See the Northern Lights
4.
5.
6.
7.
8.
9.
10.
11.
12.
13.
14.
15.
16.

17.
18.
19.
20.
21.
22.
23.
24.
25.
26.
27.
28.
29.
30.

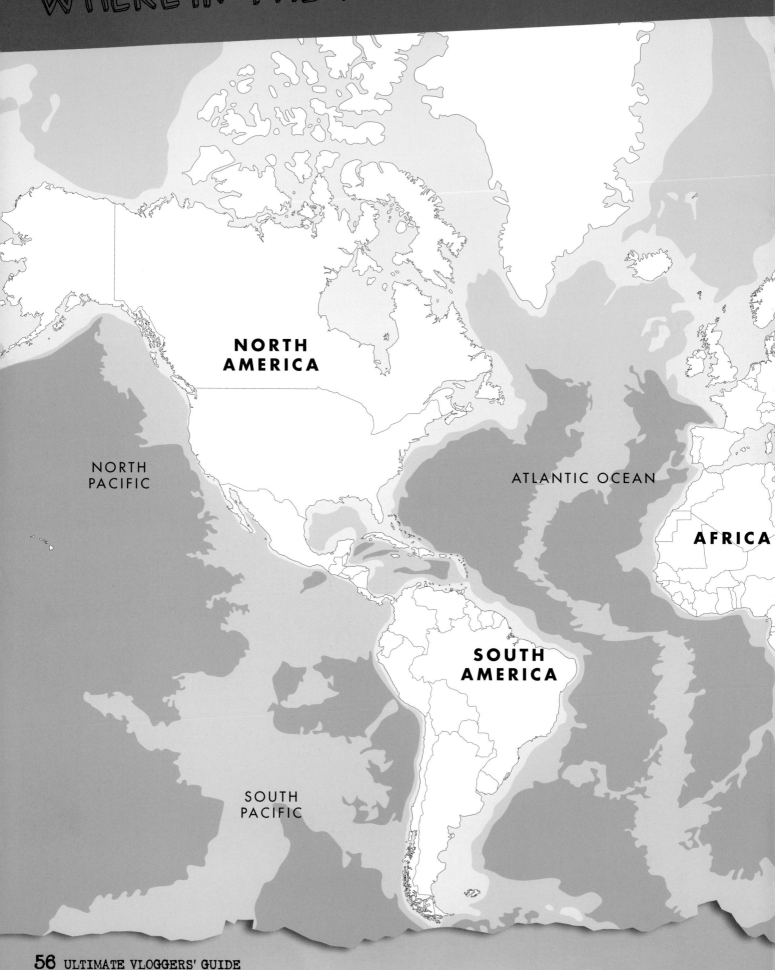

NORTH
AMERICA

NORTH
PACIFIC

ATLANTIC OCEAN

AFRICA

SOUTH
AMERICA

SOUTH
PACIFIC

Grab some colouring pencils.
Colour in the places you've been one
colour and the places you dream of
visiting another colour and start
making your travel plans.

EUROPE

ASIA

PACIFIC
OCEAN

AUSTRALIA

INDIAN OCEAN

GLOBAL YOUTUBE EVENTS

Imagine if you could just jump on a jet and attend every single YouTube event and meet up? See if you can guess where these events take place.

PLAYLIST LIVE

This event launched in 2011 and takes place twice a year. With a focus on all Internet creators including YouTube and Vine, Playlist attracts stars from all around the world including Jenna Marbles, Louis Cole and Troye's little bro Tyde Levi.

Where in the world? ....

SUMMER IN THE CITY

Surprisingly this event takes place during the summer! It's the biggest YouTube event in this country and had humble beginnings in 2009 when a group of YouTubers planned a small three-day event in the capital's parks. With panels, performances and meet-ups, this is the place to be.

Where in the world? ....

ITATUBE

There's a clue in the title of this homegrown YouTube convention, which attracts creators from across the globe. With duo-lingual panels and meet-ups, fans from this country get to meet stars and fellow YouTube fanatics.

Where in the world? ....

AMPLIFY LIVE

This celebration of YouTube is a two-hour live show featuring the world's biggest YouTube stars. It takes place in seven cities across this enormous country and offers fans the chance to meet and greet YouTube stars including Troye Sivan, Eva Gutowski and Connor Franta.

Where in the world? ....

Turn to page 62 for the answers.

VIDYOU

This country has a very passionate YouTube community. Thousands of locals and not-so-locals flock to this summer event to talk all things YouTube. VidYou also runs an awards gala during the event where fans can vote for their faves.

Where in the world? ....

VIDEODAYS

This event is the biggest independent YouTube event that takes place not only in this country, but on the continent! With two events planned in two cities in 2017, VideoDays promises its 20,000+ visitors meet-ups, performances and events with big YouTube stars.

Where in the world? ....

TUBECO

TubeCo is a huge celebration of YouTube which is more like a festival than an event. With live shows, meet-and-greets, panels, contests, live gaming and crazy challenges, this is a must-attend event for the passionate YouTube community of this area.

Where in the world? ....

CRAICCON

This fun-filled festival is a place for fans to make new friends, whether you're a subscriber or a creator. They promise collaboration, creation, education and even pizza! What started out with around 75 content creators meeting in 2014 is growing into an event that promises to be huge!

Where in the world? ....

ORLANDO.US

MILAN.ITALY

DUBLIN.IRELAND

AUSTRALIA

PORTUGAL

BERLIN.GERMANY

HELSINKI.FINLAND

LONDON.UK

THE BEST OF THE REST

Some vlogger's don't fit neatly into boxes (have you ever tried putting AmazingPhil in a box?). Here are our favourite vloggers who deserve an honourable mention!

CONNORFRANTA
NAME: Connor Joel Franta
SUBSCRIBERS: +5.5 million
Connor started out on YouTube as part of collab team Our2ndLife. His own channel is filled with chatter about all the things that interest him. We love that he can be funny and serious at the same time.

BFFS

Joe and Caspar lived together for over two years, and pranked each other on an almost daily basis. In February 2016 they announced that they were moving out, but reassured fans that they'd still live within walking (and pranking) distance of each other. Phew!

MARCUS BUTLER
NAME: Marcus Lloyd Butler
SUBSCRIBERS: +4.5 million
Marcus is a part time rapper and full time vlogger. He vlogs about anything from the ups and downs of his life to hilarious pranks and sketches. He's good friends with Alfie Deyes and the pair often attempt to break world records together!

BFFS

JOEY GRACEFFA
NAME: Joey Michael Graceffa
SUBSCRIBERS: +6.3 million
Joey vlogs daily whether he's gaming, being funny, making a parody, showing off his amazing singing skills or just updating us on his life. It must be exhausting being so awesome, but Joey makes it look easy!

Dan and Phil are BFFs who can achieve anything together, whether it's hosting a radio show, drawing cat whiskers on one another or launching the 7-second challenge app. The pair are affectionately known as 'Phan' by their fans!

MY FAVE VLOGGERS

Fill these profiles with your favourite vloggers. Add a picture, write in their channel name and write about why you love them.

Username:

Real name:

Twitter name:

Instagram name:

What they vlog about:

Why I love them:

Username:

Real name:

Twitter name:

Instagram name:

What they vlog about:

Why I love them:

Username:

Real name:

Twitter name:

Instagram name:

What they vlog about:

Why I love them:

ANSWERS

Page 11
Lifestyle Word Search

```
Q V O H E X E R C I S E H O I
F M R E E U E Q W F I J Q R F
R M O L E Q J I D H E L P Q I
I K F T O S L U L F G B P G T
E C U C I P O T C B F Q I I N
N Z N Q C V V C H D K K N R E
D R E L A X A T I O N I E Q S
S Z F T Y H Y T K O R N S E S
H V V Q L S J Q I O L G S R O
I F S N S W Q E Q O V L B S L
P B N J U H W U U Z N F I U Q
L V N U T R I T I O N E W F R
G L N U R H F O L I V I N G E
N D I W L K Y L N I H P L P X
H N N E N T H U S I A S M T O
```

Page 14
True or False?

1. false (it's called 'Teehee'),
2. true, 3. true, 4. false (he always
made comedy vids), 5. true, 6. false
(they're called #higaholics), 7. true,
8. true.

Page 27
Match the Stats

1. 33%, 2. 40+ minutes, 3. 840
million+, 4. 80%, 5. 400+ hours,
6. 50%, 7. 63%, 8. 88.

Page 33
VLOGGING CROSSWORD

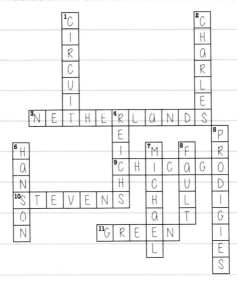

Page 46
Let's Play Word Search

```
F O M E M S N S R R D P T P O
S T A R C R A F T E O U Q O E
B S L S H M Q N D S O C V R R
Q G K Q T K M E M L N B D T F
N P L Y K E T Y L S I I Q Q H
H O H G R R Q S G N O K L J
E N Q M Q I F O Y T F S C Y P
W G K H M U M E I N O H H I D
P Q C M Q N K H W D X O F Q C
P N U F G N E P E M S C I Z V
U E I O O Y Z E G D Q K Z E Q
O J U D O N K E Y K O N G L I
O G E B R Z R O C K B A N D S
P O K E M O N O P H B S S Q R
```

Page 52
Lyrics Quiz

1. Make a rainbow with the sky,
Then wipe you it 'till it's dry.
2. But we can stay here, And laugh
away the fear.

3. But mermaids are going missing,
They end up in someone's stew.
4. I just want to see the stars with
you.
5. And yet somehow still forty winks
elude me.

Page 53
True or False?

1. false (there's a cello too),
2. false (Tom Fletcher plays the
guitar in McFly), 3. true, 4. true,
5. false (Colleen Ballinger created
Miranda to be talentless), 6. false
(his second YT song about ex-
girlfriends has over 11 million views),
7. false (she was voted off in the
quarter finals), 8. false (she plays
the ukulele).

Page 59
Global YouTube Events

Playlist Live - Orlando, US

ITATube - Milan, Italy

Summer in the City - London, UK

Amplify Live - Australia

VidYou - Portugal

TubeCo - Helsinki, Finland

VideoDays - Berlin (and Cologne),
Germany

CraicCon - Dublin, Ireland